# BITTER IN THE BELLY

T0096361

THE HUGH MacLENNAN POETRY SERIES
Editors: Allan Hepburn and Carolyn Smart

TITLES IN THE SERIES

# Bitter in the Belly

JOHN EMIL VINCENT

McGill-Queen's University Press
Montreal & Kingston • London • Chicago

© John Emil Vincent 2021

ISBN 978-0-2280-0907-8 (paper)
ISBN 978-0-2280-1031-9 (ePDF)
ISBN 978-0-2280-1032-6 (ePUB)

Legal deposit fourth quarter 2021
Bibliothèque nationale du Québec

Printed in Canada on acid-free paper that is 100% ancient forest free
(100% post-consumer recycled), processed chlorine free

 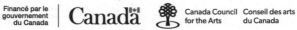

Funded by the Government of Canada    Financé par le gouvernement du Canada

Canada Council for the Arts    Conseil des arts du Canada

We acknowledge the support of the Canada Council for the Arts.

Nous remercions le Conseil des arts du Canada de son soutien.

---

Library and Archives Canada Cataloguing in Publication

Title: Bitter in the belly / John Emil Vincent.

Names: Vincent, John Emil, 1969– author.

Series: Hugh MacLennan poetry series.

Description: Series statement: The Hugh MacLennan poetry series |
Poems.

Identifiers: Canadiana (print) 20210284129 | Canadiana (ebook)
20210284137 | ISBN 9780228009078 (paper) |
ISBN 9780228010319 (ePDF) | ISBN 9780228010326 (ePUB)

Classification: LCC PS3622.I545 B58 2021 | DDC 811/.6—dc23

---

This book was typeset by Marquis Interscript in 9.5/13 Sabon.

In memoriam


Brian Selsky

and

José Esteban Muñoz

The past grabs back
what it lets us handle

To always mourn
one solution

Never to
another

Or
sing along:

dogs tuning
to sirens

CONTENTS

BITTER IN THE BELLY

# AT THE TEMPLE

*O lastly over-strong against thyself!*
Milton, *Samson Agonistes*

His hands slip up the pillars
His bare feet stutter, slide.

From here he looks drawn
and quartered

on his own hard yawn.

\*   \*   \*

If we hadn't already been
we would have stood –

Laughing, clapping him into what topples by outliving
   temples:
Myth – who hitched to time – has it made.

\*   \*   \*

For now though
he shouts unheard.

Adam's apple –
a thumb knuckle

soothing a bird.

At this fountain
the sailor can think only
to piss the surface clean of reflection.

      The care with which his fingers
      free the necessary part
      seems promising for him as a lover.

The moon shatters, shatters, buckles,
shakes itself out and reappears
nonchalant.

      Tucked back in, he's too much yours,
      a mere extra in your movie
      snagging the prop bourbon from the pool's ledge.

"Look," he points, as he drapes
his bottle-weighted arm around your neck:
its reflection rests on the crest of that moon.

      You become a face next to his
      on the breathing belly of the water;
      a hip that gives to his hip; eyes locked on themselves.

You want him and his eye for detail right there:
where need and willingness meet
at one forceful point

      so only their disturbance shows.

# NEAR NOTHING

So little happened that afternoon,
car doors, a walk, cigarettes –

the near nothing
of pleasure:

soft push
of a palm-folded earlobe.

My skin squirrelled you away
as pines do wind.

But with dusk,
our leavetaking:

patchy light,
as if from pressed,

uncovered eyes.
The moon climbing the trees

crotch upon crotch.
What words unwedged

from our silhouettes?
All I can recall:

the peepers,
the greening of the pond,

the gristle-rubbing crickets.

Nakedness derives from stone.

The watercarved armpit,
independent life of the belly.

Heritage from cramp.

The hint (from quiet genitals) –
beauty: from desire, stilled.

Always scale; grim comparison.

How envious the past
surfacing for revenge,

these eyeless fish
in sunlit pools.

Proud shapes
poised in foolish sacrifice.

# IDOL

The sky takes its first drag of sun,
the mist shakes its coat.

Your standing form remains
a piece of night, backlit
bitten into waking glare.

When noon is piled on the air,
your shadow down around your ankles –
the breathless sky
will kneel before you.

## NAY, HE HATH NEED OF NAUGHT!
## HE IS A WISE MAN!

Immortality but not youth,
fame without copyright,
living in a castle corner
the rest cordoned for tours –

> Gilgamesh,
> two-thirds god knew
> all he did writ itself in stone
> but would outlast him:
> he was, that is to say, humbled
> by his own greatness.

Enkidu, his best friend,
someone he could *barely*
beat up, tried to talk him
out of lasting longer

> by dying faster: he said,
> *in my dream, the hand that opens the gate*
> *goes weak.*

In *my* dream, the reply,
our corpses are dragged
and dumped in a pile.
Heroes are scared
sacred:

> Legend's a brazier

which gutters in the cold wind,
a back door which opens only

      to squall and storm,

a battering ram
reversed by the enemy,

      a crippling shoe.
      All's paradox: predictable, sad.

Enkidu: why does your heart speak strangely?

I tire of this, says Gilgamesh,
stamp me in gold already.

*

Those eyes crouched on your pile of features
like mouths.

       Our path past the bicycle spokes
       shot through with a streetlamp's spines.

A staircase complaining
in almost perfect scales.

       The bed, cigarettes,
       hands.

My head a stone eagle
over the entrance to a mine.

Raised far from rivers I didn't know
smooth sheets of motion. Things stopped and after:
became their stillness. Days ran into months and
   disappeared,
the calm of any plural threatened. Once
I dreamt I, as e e cummings, steadier of hummingbirds,
rode a twister, a long fading moan;
I bucked roofs,
they flew clean as circumflexes from telegrams.
Row upon row, block by block what I knew came visible.
I chomped into basements
expecting boxes of wigged, dead heads.
Instead: I found – buried! – stacks of photos –
pictures of fountains, pictures of rivers.

In the parking lot
one boy tells another:

*I could love you.*

He'll turn away from the window,
and tomorrow he'll make a note:

*Never plead in earshot.*

## ABANDONED WAREHOUSE
## IN THE AFTERNOON


Near its entrance, a bird peeps renditions
Of the shape and sharpness of its beak.
                    Around, trees stripped
                    To snags of wire.

The high windows
Concede to the winded day
                    Only squared-off shafts
                    And shrugs of rags.

Tonight it will be charted
By constellations of cigarettes;
                    Tonight within these walls:
                    A low clear sky without a moon.

Men snipped from balloons of speech
Will gather, lean on oil drums, against girders –
                    I cannot say that even now
                    I am not filled with that nothing.

I imagine playing
In this puppet theatre
                    Whose only characters
                    Are clacks of limbs:

My heart pumps
Klepto-fast and my eyes
                    Jag over a dark depiction
                    Of fear and lust, or, fearless, hate.

But the wind shuffles cables slung from rafters.
A crow calls.

                    In the light I've met no one,
                    Leave with a sigh, not safety.

## AQUEDUCT

I dropped into you
to hear the deep

bass crack
of ice,

faults born while substance
changes phases.

But things did not break:

the truth barrelling through
a badly told lie.

The lie lingered.

Because I was not ice,
I was stone.

Your finger
bumping

down
my spine

in smooth
ellipses

I.

Then came a day when returning
became not possible
but irresistible.
If memory bit,
this chewed.

The rains,
each sheet discrete,
bar-coded on asphalt.

I saw your beard
worm into you.

Eyes brighter in rewind,
your wince a smeared smile.

I should perhaps have smiled back.

II.

The castle on the hill
means siege.

Your wet dad planted
your dry mom
mid-vineyard.

And the bad people
escaped

barely

by inflicting themselves
till nothing remained of them.

You became their memory,
they beckoned you back.

You stopped talking,
they begged.

Because they knew
from begging.

How it repels.

III.

The empty glass display box
your family is.

Mystery of nothing:
we came again and again

to it

wondering at, no,
refusing to believe the lovelessness.

Stubborn,
we insisted: life over time

weighs. Cruelty
has correlative; coldness, motive.

Hands,
more than grip.

IV.

The dogs' bones
in their basket

sometimes
gnawed sawed ends:

evidence of brutality.

The bones
they nosed, toys.

Some days, worse,
toys.

V.

This is apology. For wrongs
done you. Because I can.

Except mine. Those, or,
that, was never to see what

the basket held. To refuse
rewind. That

we'd've lasted mere months
without translation into dog.

CLEAR CUT

Strange.
While I was chopping
there was plenty of shade . . .

Porcupines
emerge, dustballs at an estate sale,
their cries are baby cries.

I forget its name,
but it's half-otter
half-human, calls from the forest
in the voice of someone you love,
someone you love in trouble.

Amid log smell
and saw leavings puffed to oyster crackers,
in the drizzle, I hear it still.

That thing,
it'll lure you into the forest.
I mean: metaphorically.

Asleep, or ecstatic, let them be.
Faces topographical with pleasure.

They've been. And seen.
Too soon. But not too late.

Their eyes don't roll up
when their lids click closed.

Spare them knowing
knowing won't spare them.

## THAT THEY MAY UPHOLD
## HIM HORIZONTALLY

Little Hans naps, face pressed
to the couch pillow's button
– he'll have to be carried up.

But what he wants:

To be too heavy
but *still* to have to be carried –
*fame* he thinks. *Like fame.*

Blessed are the famous,
loved and unmoved.

Huddled,
if only there were opposition proper.

They could take it;
there's nothing they couldn't accept.

\* \* \*

They should be strong,
like a march

but there's the baton league
and the flags

to wait through
before the message.

And there's TV,
and what's on.

And feeling not very good,
and just not social.

Gratitude for a lasagna
sent two months ago.

Strong loyalty: the kind
that's a warning.

\* \* \*

O, may the peace of empty benches
overtake you mis-designed souls.

You were not meant to be born,
and meant

not to act on it.

# TRICK

The moon with his soft charcoal jockey's cap
pulled low . . . clouds of night jasmine.

Between us: a country. But tonight
as if on fans' up-pressing hands I could be carried
I suspect, like a rock star
to you.

Night and crickets. They aren't
stitching on old Singers. Rather:
unzipping, then zipping back up. The gown scene
before any grand ball, but repeated relentlessly
and could it be
stuck enough
in that moment –
reflected in the pivoting wood-framed mirror –
that these are perfectly round plates
twirling on poles,
where, there is so little of me left,
I could walk to you.

# ULCER

Joke
or lesson:

spit-up blood's
callcd

"coffee grounds."
And against

porcelain – sugared

Turkish dregs: startling-
ly correct.

Joke
or lesson:

that one
always comes back

forcibly

as the other.

When the soul
scootches around
in the bucket seat
of body.

When tree lines
draw their curtains
and the river's
quizzical.

There's a fist
trying to be made
in my chest –
quivering,

which is,
the heart insists
to the disagreeable head,
at least

a gesture.

What are you doing here? Ordinary men are hacking
other ordinary men, exquisitely, in half.

Your friends, could they, in uniform,
point the way, ladies and gentlemen, to the gas?

The thickets you'll scratch and scrape through
aren't nightmares. Worse: they aren't nightmares.

# SAINT ANTHONY

Dithering. Can it be that old age
*is* sainthood – mortal acts,
dirt worn off the artifact?

Slumped. I can see
just where they'll cut
for relics.

Anthony, your goodness:

it waits to rip you to pieces.

People like us –
educated out of importance –
can *mourn*
or *yearn*.

Thirty, unemployed,
I thought the world
had turned its back. But
*I* had – so not to suffer its loss.

You were braced against the gale;
the way was steep.
You trained; you rowed
on a machine at home.

What you want I'm sad you can't have.
It's a time after the humiliations:
a time of triumphs. And the poets prove:
a time after ours.

# STORY

First she thought
That Could Be Me

then
Thank God It's Not.

But it followed her
from the breakroom.

The drill press
made repeated suggestions

the card clock
stapled it to her sleeve.

Surely everyone else saw it,
thought it a remnant of her neglect.

The clerk snagged her cigarettes
from above his head without looking

he bagged the tampons
quickly, left the gum on the counter.

Why an escaped dwarf?
Why an unrealistic family

each behind
a curtain opened

at the touch of a button?
Her Datsun hunkered.

Inside, the smell of new heat.
The roads swallowed snow.

And the front door

was unlocked.
But she only read it

that afternoon,
after leaving the Cheerios

toppled and spilled
over the spare key.

She must have left all the lights on
on purpose, the shower dripping,

every window open,
an icicle on the bathroom faucet

shy and shiny as a tear.
The shower curtain

pulled full around.
The heat clanked to catch up.

Closing each window,
latching each window

she recalled sidestepping
the centre of the hallway,

stepping around it.
No mark.

But she stepped around it
again, understood

something missing.
The end of the story was unconvincing

though, revenge is never zip-locked,

it is what starts stories
and the dead always come back

as earaches or missing buttons.
Putting the kettle on

felt epic,
pulling the teabag

from its sleeve,
definitive.

The salt and pepper shakers
were each toppled

next to a knife out of the block.
She'd forgot her trip to the bank,

she'd forgot dinner,
she'd hurried past the clogged

mail box.
The setting wasn't even convincing.

But now one spool unravelled,
its thread stabbed

into canvas, in rows.
Formed a sack.

Rocks rimmed
the dead herbs

out back. They clacked
in the sack, sound of boats

at dock. The hatchback
groaned open.

The bag curled perfectly
around the spare.

The drive was short,
the lake frozen.

Hard to chip.
Now and then the boom

of great plates
suturing.

Then there was a hole.
The sack slid into it

like oil,
and the shattered ice

rippled back,
little floes

rocked and settled,
as if a puzzle done

just to do a puzzle
for the hundredth time.

She smoked all the way home.

Where was the circus now?
Who had a circus

in the dead of winter?
In what trailer

did occupants persist
on bourbon and canned sausages?

It wasn't hers, the story,
but she worked at it,

and shifting on her seat
a necklace snagged the seat belt

a necklace she'd never seen before
plopped its beads

in her lap.

## WEED

I thought: lacy.
You show me blood.

Tiny queen collar
neck stub.

Or: hanky
in uncanny hands

after dabbing the stump.

Or: the fatal
cough.

The mark –
trillion on the hill.

Over her face they laid it;
she was not yet dead.

Or a cardinal,
a cloud.

Trillion on the hill,
on the frown of hill.

Blizzard stoplight, bottle base,
wedding sheet . . .

And the lace moon,
full curtsy.

Which, I wonder,
better?

You insist the flower.
You say, the moon's

not even *pretty*:

a pocked hotel hallway ashtray –
it's not beautiful.

Not beautiful:
just far away.

I understand the beasts.
They mean only harm.

Stay, but when you hear
the blood feast: run

and then stand
right where

my cries
turn demands.

## UNA CHUPACABRITA

He sits in the hand
Like a gun meant for a purse.

His crest, his seahorse tail.
His greenish almost scaled skin.

To be dead means to be identified.
Or at least no longer a mystery.
So they all think.

In that dinosaur saw blade skull
Digits are still turning to goats
And goats to cows and cows
To fountains.
                    As sort of
Beautiful as a wedding
Ice sculpture, but faster in melting.
Sweet creature, how can incipience
Not be innocent, or no, how can fierceness
In its earliest form not be celebrity,
How can we leave these little eared
Seahorse mermaid blood sucking legends
To die alone. We also die a little.
We are either fountains
Or thirsts. We are stone-walled
Pools or the weird young people who
Stomp around on cool nights
I guess drunk
And splash one another

And think that this is innocence,
When it is una chupacabrita,
Incipience, violence, calm.
Play with your handgadgets,
Walk with your head down.
But know, children, kids,
Near adults, something is younger
Yet. And curled in a warm hand and if we can do it
Brought back, and yawning, and hungry.
We'll feed it things from banks
Of freezers. And best to think
It is not just where we end,
But a place we never leave.
Chupacabrita, the life we used
To give you was as ranchers,
We had valuables grazing.
Now, sweet thing, we are the valuables,
When you grow, know we can't
Blame anything for anything,
We've lost the footing
To period that sentence.
And dear thing, perhaps you will
Kill me, or someone I love,
Perhaps you are wayward nature,
Or an eye-infected driver,
Or a jerk with something to prove,
But as all these, I do love you still,
Can I love you still, curly-tailed beast,
Funny seahorse, prose poem of creatures.
I will love you. With you grown and curled
Over a donkey, a dead donkey,
Whose face was so big it was
Only comparable to a moon,

Whose face was so skully
It got human, because like humans
With hollows, it looked both hungry
Because thoughtful and the other
Way round. I could watch you
Do what you will do, should you grow
And I might chase you for football fields
But still, know, it is only part of you
I chase but the whole of you runs.

## THE WHOLE FIRMAMENT THAT
## TURNED EVEN AS WE TURNED

You were the exception when you didn't feel one.

You
        you

were about to speak
        we sat
                in the dark

the reel
        stubborn –
                through the square

window
        clicks
                and curses.

You were telling me
        you were the spirits'
                favourite

in all the cult.

        I loved the line
                between

belief
        and
                dismissal

or rather
        the line
                which is

true belief.

        The voices
                you spoke

broke over
        against you
                but one

always took
        guided –
                I saw:

a scout troop
        blindfolds
                held hands

the electric touch
        of each
                to each

thought: snake
        skeleton
                thought:

bullet train
        tradition
                thought:

would I were
         so convincing
                  amid candles.

You were
         always speaking
                  abandoned

in company.
         Toward no spot.
                  But for wending

and you
         you
                  took my silence

correctly.
         Months later
                  we'd part

badly
         after tragedy
                  and crazed reply

to tragedy
         that is
                  cruelty

to the crazed.
         But now
                  in the thick

telling
    about being
        the medium of choice

my
    what was it
        suspension

of something –
    when you fell
        silent

were going to tell
    me about
        how it felt

because I asked
    you paused
        I think: thought

and as your
    mouth opened
        the screen

lit up.

# JOB

It's no EMT's
        job
                to clean

the scene.
        Nor
                the 911

not to leave
        one.
                I said

You must go.
        Check.
                After the failed calls

after the threats.
        Took wheedling
                'til four.

He could've won
        if you hadn't
                you could've.

*How I regret*
        *it* next morning
                you

his camera in hand
            recording
                        his blood and spit

on the kitchen
            floor
                        to develop

on recovery or what
            resembled
                        recovery.

Soon after
he'd threaten
                        to kill you.

I don't think it was
            Pictures – :
                        gestures

planted that seed.
            I
                        won't blame

either of you
            stuck
                        in frames

too big
            or
                        frames

too small
        for
                psychopaths.

Needed
        a
                corkboard was my thought.

But you were my friend
        not
                him

I forgave you
        even
                when

he told you
        he'd
                kill you

forgave you
        even
                then.

Two friends almost simultaneously
Convert, telling me each that he
Intends to tattoo the fact on his chest
With a Red Cross. Saying it's the best

Symbol for possibility.
Ambulance and ampersand.
Treasure, target. Worn on white bands
By stretcher bearers. Complicity

Of the Swiss: "neutrality" and timing.
Outlasting
Its own prediction. Hot gushing
Life corralled by a tiled floor's grouting.

Slick red x of an unstaunched, bandaged wound.
But also, how hope can be, is, pronounced: And?

phantom limbs
of limbs not lost

      rooms
      open blooms

      of their chairs

      an attic beckons
      with creaking

      mannequin fingers

          – kindly enough

      a basement
      unties the shoe

      of its must

      a bathroom
      sincere

      from its placid
      rheumy eye

      while walls IV drip
      light to lamps

How to thank
the terrible dream

the anklebone
pillow

for this house
turned away from the world

How to shake
misfortune's hand

      clasped white

at the small
of its back.

# TENT

Cortázar once wrote
that happiness makes
bad literature

but I wonder
as I watch you
surrounded by friends

flanked by the dogs
telling a story
about a woman visiting Tibet

who
finding it hard
to sleep

feeling like
it was time to wake
though

still dark
put her hand
on the tent's canvas

and found it
heavy and
wet

Her heat had
called
to a thousand leeches

like happiness
to fate, always
the unsent

delivered signal
– how alive!
how attractive

# ANGER

Mid-field there is a spout of flame.

We honour it with our dead
at whom of course we're angry.

But the living:
it is inelegant

to hate them. Why spend anything
on what you can abandon?

# THOUGHT EXPERIMENT

A man washes up on a desert island.
Next to him, the book he never read.

Mostly, he finds the characters flat,
the situations improbable.

His self slides
through the lines

like floss.
It's a book about a family

so big they people a continent.
Restless, they build ships

and subdivide the moon.
Finally – space unfashionable –

time gentrifies.
Stepping back centuries

or forward as they please.
No one is ever happy in this book.

Ancestors begin to win
all the tennis.

One boy gets
so bored

he takes poison
but his father

grounds him to the day before.
The dad is a decent man,

though, as everyone knows,
he fucks goats.

There he is
belt clanking

at his ankles.
Bliss on his face.

He was stoic
when his wife

climbed back to the treehouse
with her brother.

The man is kind. People come to him
for advice.

He begins to age, develops memories.
Giddy, he names each wrinkle.

One day he ungrounds his son,
the next, he buries him.

He builds a "real time" sanctuary,
invites people.

They watch ice teas sweat
on porch railings, keep diaries.

The goats certainly seem happy.
But the stranded man

wants to punch someone.
And in the book it is he

who does slug the goat fucker,
over and over, saying

I'll give you happy.
Yeah, I'll give you happy.

## GESTURES

Rain falling so hard
on roofs

it shatters to mist.

What is it
has the heart
to lift

the drilled garden's
flattened shoots.

The sky gestures.

The earth
spits up birds.

# FIRST SNOW

The lives that run streets
return to plumb.

I recall
the cloud cover

that eased you from your features.
The sun that fetched you.

All this weight
and bright.

The evergreens with their
weird enthusiasm.

The willows,
whips.

In the wind, whips.
And down the hill

that bare stand of elms:
the veins of a heart

to which it itself
has lost its way.

SPECIALTY FISH

On chipped ice banks,
full sprawl.
Beside steppes of fillet.

Outside scales,
in-, feathers.

Hands, un- and regloved,
unfurl each beauty.

They stink of nothing.

But heavy sound the ticking,
the clanging of the hour.

Close and closer:
something breathing
on your eyes.

Huge and tranquil.

Your vision
pinched off at its periphery
is mouth-shaped –

or
it strikes you
shaped

by one.

68

We ask ourselves if it had to happen
if it would have        despite us

and conclude
that, yes, it is convenient to think that.

We sniff through your things,
we cook your foods.

We set your table. Out of politeness
we've invited people you hated.

The friends. Look! the truth –

They are as little good to each other
as they were to you.

## JONAH, DISPLEASED WITH GOD
## FOR SPARING NINEVEH

The cup of bitterness
tastes good, he thinks.

Empties it. Are
there other cups?

Places for refills.
But the cup sits

O-mouthed
stupid as pissiness.

Night falls.

He puts the cup
in the sink

sits back down.
A pale ring

on the table's wood,
– mocking eclipse

of all he desires.
Zero

lipped
by a fish.

## AT YOUR DOOR

At your door, where
the sky one last time

sunk its hooked lung line.

At the open door,
closing it did you feel

this you've taught me:
pang swell and twitch.

Cut from a length
of light. Then

stitched.

The plane falls
from the sky –

still the moonlight
shimmers on it

the letters
on the plane

still
in language

the trees
come more

into focus –
and quickly –

they don't flinch.
There are no expressions

the world
takes

in change
until change

has passed,
until the moment

relaxes
and the world

touches its face
gingerly.

The rich are sad
They've had their troubles
Taken from them – shiny
Fingertips scale their pineapples.

The professionals are sad
They've had boredom
Taken from them – plush
Are their chairs, strained their belt-leather.

The past is sad
Dragged as it is
Behind

and

The future is sad
– all it left
– the tatters

How sit
And not feel
The heartache
Of each thing?

# FACT

Like that Monty Python cartoon where one leaf
On a tree jumps free with no explanation, but a belief
In individual action, which is shown to be a lie
When another leaf leaps from grief.

Then another follows.
Finally, the tree stands bare, it
Means the season that it joins.
And it is fact, not tragedy, suddenly, it owns.

1.

Up ahead
signboards, a closed motel:

the crescent moon
"Sleepytime" sign –

a rectangle
of extra-white

where no would go.

In 1976, three truckers

beat Teddy
post-proposition

past predicate.

*They are their punishment*
I want to think.

2.

And for Brian:
*we* were *his*.

The nailed boards
leaning by the entry

when his mom answers,
the chipped hole bored

in the pull-down door.

There is a thick pronoun

where he hung.
I walk through it

to his kitchen.

3.

What do they do
with the dead

exactly?

I wanted

to know that.
I was running

over a bridge
over a small creek,

three weeks had passed.
I imagined his body.


How it fought
what they'd done.

How it would win.

4.

After the rains
the red clay lays tracks

the sentence
of their passage

to the dirt pile
of cloud. The road

was ridden yesterday.
You can read it.

5.

They made it to town.
Nothing befell them.

Except: they laid tracks . . .
and

like every novel
this one ends:

always time
smearing its red

through a field
bigger than you.

6.

We are lastly
our names.

And: first.

In between,
something slightly less.

Maybe the light
through your dirty kitchen windows

falling into reds,
thickening,

and maybe the push
of your hand through your curls

and the disorder
of your teeth, who

sometimes laughed
themselves out

before you
could catch them.

When I say your life
was Kafkaesque, I don't mean
cramped or dim –

I mean nose-scratchingly
eloquent and pressed to a puzzle
end that argues with beauty.

# HONEY IN THE MOUTH

In a dream
you are mid-lasagna,

placing mushrooms
and saying:

*what you love will*
*be taken from you*

*eras and music you like*
*that once spilled onto the esplanade*

*trimmed with chatter*
*and happiness –*

*they will pass.*
*And with them*

*sorrow.*
You foil the dish.

Set it in the oven,
unmitt, sit.

In the dream,
I'm happy,

but also *furious* with you
for planning

a dinner at my house
and refusing to come.

*But that's why*
you say *this night*

*is different*
*from all others.*

*Horseradish and honey*
*on the same plate.*

I can't argue.
It's funny and unfair:

to quote me
quoting you.

Lonely,
I read and read

the last thing you read.

Afternoon tugs,
evening plies.

Morning
has its leash in its mouth.

\* \* \*

Two chairs face:
sea swells

pelicans.
I sit watch.

The sea waiting
to poach the sun.

\* \* \*

Here I am with my hand
palm up between our chairs.

I do know that
some time ago

yours hovered
wanting to settle there.

He's youngish,
about the age you'll always be.

Up to him
he'd also have left nothing

but friends.
And with them, photos.

This one in
a black bathing costume,

arms akimbo
and a neck, the V

holds up that smile
like a crab,

wide, to prove
mastery.

\* \* \*

Spit up there,
posing,

you'd have pulled
back your hair

like Garbo,
as if to say:

Brian,
he's not here right now,

but if you think back to Garbo,
young,

you'll know
how long

he's been gone.

# YOM KIPPUR

October twilight:

a solitary walker,
blocks down,

scissors his legs
toward

and away.

Now I've known you
twice as long dead.

As taken
God bait.

And my eyes have
adjusted –

*saturated*:

your death ends,
and you push through.

Sleepy after the sun
      the house is full of light
            spilt from our eyes
                        until our eyes are empty
               and we see

ACKNOWLEDGMENTS

poems in this manuscript first appeared in these venues
sometimes in slightly different forms

*The Beloit Poetry Journal*
        "Abandoned warehouse in the afternoon"
        "Clear cut"
        "Tent"

*The Cortland Review*
        "Anger"

*Denver Quarterly*
        "Una Chupacabracita" [now "Una Chupacabrita"]

*Drunken Boat*
        "Thought experiment"
        "Story"
        "The cup of bitterness" [now "Jonah, displeased
          with God for sparing Nineveh"]
        – finalists for the *Drunken Boat* Panliterary Awards

*failbetter*
        "The Closed Eyes of the Ravished"
        "In the shadow, in the house"

*The Gay & Lesbian Review Worldwide*
        "Near nothing"

*Gents, Bad Boys, and Barbarians: New Gay Poets*
   (anthology)
               " * "

               "Idol"
               "Abandoned warehouse in the afternoon"
               "Young man and sailor"

*The James White Review*
               "Young man and sailor"

*Liberty Hill Poetry Review*
               "+" [now "Positive"]

*The Massachusetts Review*
               "The evening"

*The Plum Review*
               "Raised far from rivers"
               "Untitled" [now " * "]

*Spinning Jenny*
               "The Island of Misfit Toys"